SpringerBriefs in Business

More information about this series at http://www.springer.com/series/8860

Gabriel Steinhardt

Market-Value Pricing

Definitions, Concepts, and Processes for Market-Value Centric Pricing

Springer

Gabriel Steinhardt
Blackblot
Caesarea, Israel

ISSN 2191-5482 ISSN 2191-5490 (electronic)
SpringerBriefs in Business
ISBN 978-3-030-10733-8 ISBN 978-3-030-10734-5 (eBook)
https://doi.org/10.1007/978-3-030-10734-5

Library of Congress Control Number: 2018966593

This Springer imprint is published by the registered company Springer Nature Switzerland AG
The registered company address is: Gewerbestrasse 11, 6330 Cham, Switzerland

Foreword

This book will help those responsible for making pricing decisions, both within a business setting and privately, understand the various considerations that impact the pricing process. It will aid in the efforts to price a product with a novel, clear, and structured process.

For over 7 years I have assisted Gabriel Steinhardt in his development of the product management body of knowledge, specifically the *Blackblot Product Manager's Toolkit*® (PMTK) product management methodology. This no-frills book which focuses solely on pricing is an extension of that previous effort.

The primary purpose of the *Blackblot Market-Value Pricing*™ *Model* (MVP Model), which is introduced in this book, is to help companies and individuals become more successful in their product pricing efforts. With the release of this book, it is hoped that pricing will be demystified and viewed as a structured task.

This book provides the tools, concepts, and knowledge to perform pricing, but ultimately, it is up to the individual to make the actual product pricing decisions. Pricing is all about making business decisions, not mathematical calculations. There are no magic formulas for pricing.

Without the burden of overbearing analytical verbiage and with the intent of promoting readability, this intentionally succinct and practical book aims to provide readers with the knowledge and tools to partake in pricing activities in an organized and efficient way.

Daniel Stadler

Acknowledgments

Without the help and support of some very special people, my work and this book would have never become a reality.

Daniel Stadler, a product management expert and technology business advisor, has been providing me with insight, suggestions, critical review, commentary, advice, guidance, and support for many years, including in the development of the *Blackblot Market-Value Pricing™ Model* (MVP Model). A special note of gratitude is extended to him for his invaluable contribution.

My sincere thanks go to all my business partners, fellow instructors, and students worldwide whose feedback and creativity has challenged me. They have candidly shared their thoughts, and I have gained much from each of them. I am grateful for their continued support.

I am also thankful to the ever-professional editorial staff at Springer-Verlag and their partners who have contributed to this literary project. This book was made possible by the diligent work of Amelia Winkle, Dan Stadler, Karen Higgins, Christian Rauscher, and Philipp Baun.

Finally, I thank Professor Yael Hanein for her help, commitment, patience, perseverance, faith, support, and love in the life journey she has accompanied me on so far. Without her I would not be where I am today.

Gabriel Steinhardt

Introduction

Pricing is the act of setting a price, and *Price* is defined as the specification of what a seller wants in exchange for granting right of ownership or use to a product.

The *marketing mix* is a popular framework for marketing management decisions. The marketing mix (originally referred to as the 4Ps) describes a combination of variables (Product/Price/Promotion/Place) which are controlled by a company in an attempt to influence customers to purchase its products.

Price is the only marketing mix variable that is directly related to producing revenue. Without revenue to facilitate cash flow, the short-term lifeblood of any business, the business quickly withers away and becomes unviable. All other marketing mix variables represent costs and are indirectly related to producing revenue.

Consequently, pricing a product is one of the most important and most challenging of business decisions. It is a strategic task that is based on complex information and numerous fluctuating and interrelated factors.

The challenge with pricing is that it is intrinsically inexact, probabilistic, and unpredictable. There is no single best pricing mechanism. The pricing process and the resulting price vary over time, location, commodity, financial situation, market conditions, and more.

Pricing a product is an elusive and fraught effort. There must always be the sober realization that there are no guaranteed results and pricing may be frustrating at times, but it is crucial to success (commercial and otherwise). Yet it is possible to reduce the risks of failure at all levels (financial, marketing, technology) and increase the chances of success with a structured approach.

Pricing is an ever-changing and ongoing process. It is like a game of chess: ambiguous, lacking in necessary details, and without clear "right" answers. An incorrect pricing decision can be impactful with a spectrum of adverse financial and marketing consequences. A correct pricing decision can have immensely positive and far-reaching implications on a business, particularly on profit and brand.

In response to this challenge, this book introduces the *Blackblot Market-Value Pricing™ Model* (MVP Model), a market-value centric pricing process which guides sets of managerial decisions that help determine a product's price.

This book delineates useful concepts, models, and processes that aid the making of actual pricing decisions, and its goal is to help those responsible for pricing to be able to effectively engage in product pricing activities.

Contents

About the Author

Gabriel Steinhardt is Blackblot's founder and CEO and a recognized international technology product management expert, author, lecturer, and developer of practical tools and methodologies that increase product managers' productivity.

A marketing and information systems MBA with over two decades of experience in product management with technology products, Gabriel has assumed diverse leadership roles with major corporations and start-ups in marketing, product management, and technical undertakings.

Gabriel is the developer of the *Blackblot Product Manager's Toolkit*® (PMTK) product management methodology, a globally adopted best practice.

Chapter 1
Pricing Fundamentals

1.1 Introduction

This section contains key concepts and ideas to build the necessary foundational knowledge which will be employed in the pricing process.

1.2 Pricing Definitions

Pricing is the act of setting a price. *Price* is defined as the specification of what a seller wants in exchange for granting right of ownership or use to a product.

Do not confuse price with payment. *Payment* is defined as the actual economic sacrifice a customer makes to acquire certain rights to a product. Sometimes, there is a difference between the stated price and the payment, which represents what the customer ultimately gives the seller to acquire usage or ownership rights to the product.

One other related term is *Costing*. When you go through the process of costing, you determine the monetary value of resources that are used when you produce goods or provide a service. Through the costing process, you arrive at *Cost*, which is defined as the monetary value of the aforementioned resources.

In this book, *Costs* can refer to either the manufacturer's cost or the consumer's cost. Unless otherwise noted, the differentiation is noted next to the term (i.e. Costs_m for the manufacturer's costs and Costs_c for the consumer's costs).

1.3 Price Formula

The price formula is basic and intuitive:

G. Steinhardt, *Market-Value Pricing*, SpringerBriefs in Business,
https://doi.org/10.1007/978-3-030-10734-5_1

$$\text{Price} = \text{Costs}_{\text{m}} + \text{Margins}$$

So, to arrive at the price, you add the Costs_{m} and Margins. A manufacturer's Costs_{m} include all expenses incurred by the manufacturer for manufacturing, distributing, marketing, and selling the product.

The *Margins* are the direct financial gains of selling. Many companies use the term margin/s interchangeably with the term markup. A *Markup* and a *Markdown* are, by true definition, any increase or reduction in the price of an item from its initially established price.

1.4 Pricing Definition Example

Following is a fictitious example to illustrate pricing fundamental concepts. Apple's design team has created a new iPhone model. Apple's project team goes through the costing process. For each new iPhone, they estimate the following resources:

Resources	Cost
Materials	$200
Labor	$200
Shipping	$100
Marketing	$200

When you sum all these resources, you find that the total cost of each new iPhone is $700.

Apple's product management team determines that they want a margin of $300 for each iPhone. Based on the price formula of **Price** = **Costs_{m}** + **Margins**, they determine that the price for each iPhone should be $1000.

Apple begins manufacturing, marketing, and selling the new iPhone. After a year, Apple determines that it is time to entice more demand for the new iPhone. Accordingly, Apple communicates a special promotion that offers the iPhone at a discounted rate of $925 for 1 month. The markdown for the iPhone in that month is $75. During this promotion, the official stated price of the iPhone remains $1000, but potential customers can actually buy the new iPhone for a payment of $925.

1.5 Price Importance

The price of a product holds a host of associated business and marketing implications. Price can exert three cardinal implications on a business. You must always take these implications into account during the pricing process:

- Price affects the product's brand image.
- Price determines the customers and the competition.

- Price determines profitability and, consequently, the potential for the company to survive.

1.6 Pricing Fundamentals Retention Drill

1. What is pricing?
   (a) The act of setting a price
   (b) The value placed on a product
   (c) The amount of money or goods
   (d) The method to price a product
2. Which is the price formula?
   (a) Price = Total Cost/(1 − Gross Margins)
   (b) Price = Costs_m − Gross Margins
   (c) Price = Costs_m + Margins
   (d) Price = Cost + Markup
3. What is a price markup?
   (a) The ratio between the cost of a product and its price
   (b) Value that is added to the cost price of a product
   (c) An increase in the price of an item from its initially established price
   (d) A common practice of adding a constant percentage to the nominal price
4. Which three implications must be taken into account during the pricing process? (multiple response)
   (a) Price leads to government taxation
   (b) Price determines profitability
   (c) Price determines the customers and the competition
   (d) Price can become a politically charged factor
   (e) Price affects the product's brand image
   (f) Price determines the product's nominal costs

Answers: 1-(a), 2-(c), 3-(c), 4-(b, c, e)

Chapter 2
Value Concept

2.1 Introduction

This section contains key concepts and ideas that explain the bilateral relationship between price and value.

2.2 Price and Value

On an intuitive level, *Value* is the worth derived by the customer from owning and using the product. The value concept is illustrated with the value formula:

$$\text{Value} = \text{Benefits} - \text{Costs}_c$$

The value formula is an intuitive formula—not mathematical. It is more of a perception and it is not a *Cost/Benefit Ratio*, a financial term which means the monetary return for each dollar invested.

In the value formula, *Benefits* consist of product features that are desirable to the customer. Costs_c are all of the expenses the customer incurs in buying and using the product. You can think of the term Costs_c as functionally similar to the idea of *Total Cost of Ownership* (*TCO*), which reflects the customer's accumulated direct and indirect costs in buying and using a product.

The customer estimates the value that the product provides by the degree of the relevant positive outcome that the product provides to the customer in proportion to the $\text{Costs}_{c.}$ The relevant positive outcome that the product provides may include, for example, cost savings, improved usability (ease of operation), streamlined business processes (improved efficiencies), the ability to perform entirely new tasks (new capabilities), automation of previously manual tasks (work automation), improved

G. Steinhardt, *Market-Value Pricing*, SpringerBriefs in Business,
https://doi.org/10.1007/978-3-030-10734-5_2

productivity (scope of useful features), or reduced rework (more productive use of time).

Although closely related, value and worth are not similar terms. *Worth* is the level of subjective usefulness or importance that the product holds for the customer. *Value* is the worth of the product in relation to $\text{Costs}_{c.}$

Estimating value is a uniquely personal and psychological judgment. For example, two people can look at the very same product and have completely opposite views of the value the product holds.

When a customer claims that a product is *not worth it*, they actually mean that the product's value is low or, more commonly, they subjectively believe that the expenditure in effort or money they invest in the product will not yield sufficient usefulness or importance in return.

For example, professional carpenters pay up to several thousand dollars for an advanced table saw, which they personally believe will allow them to improve productivity and do more complex woodworking. The carpenters believe that this type of expenditure is *worth it* for its potential. However, only the test of time will tell if buying an advanced table saw has real value which would factually materialize in the form of time saved or increased sales.

Value is something people seek and are willing to pay for. Companies employ different product delivery strategies, which manipulate the value formula in order to increase a product's value.

Consider the following:

- At a sales-driven company, the salespeople often want to lower the product's official list price or provide excessive discounts in order to increase a product's value.
- At a technology-driven company, the engineers want to inflate the product's feature set (add more benefits) in order to increase a product's value.
- At a market-driven company, the product managers build value based on what customers need, and the product's feature set is built accordingly to provide that value.

You should always seek to enhance your product's value. Educate customers to strongly consider value as the primary decision factor when buying.

2.3 Value Interdependency

There is interdependency between value, benefits, margins, price, and Costs_{m}. Because of that interdependency, the lower limit for pricing a product is the manufacturer's costs (Costs_{m}), and the upper limit is the monetary value placed on the product's features (benefits) by the customer. Clearly, you should avoid selling your product for what it costs to manufacture your product (Costs_{m}).

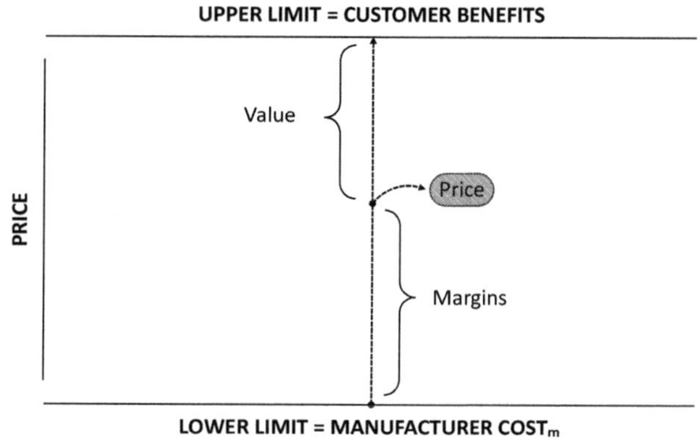

Fig. 2.1 Relationship between value, benefits, margins, price, and Costs$_m$

The actual price of the product will be anywhere between the upper and lower limits. When you set a price, you consequently also determine the margins that are afforded to the manufacturer and the value derived by the customer (Fig. 2.1).

For example, for a bakery, the Costs$_m$ to bake one artisan loaf of bread are \$3. The retail price of one loaf is \$7, and the monetary value placed on the artisan bread by the customer is \$8. Therefore, the margins afforded to the bakery are \$4, and the advantage in monetary value enjoyed by the customer is \$1.

2.4 Relative Value Concept

The *Relative Value* concept addresses the ratio between benefits and Costs$_c$. Many people express this concept of relative value by the phrase, "You get what you pay for."

This means that the more you pay, the more desirable benefits you receive, and vice versa. For example, more-features-for-more-Costs$_c$ has been traditionally considered the relative value of European products made by highly developed countries such as Switzerland or Germany. In contrast, less-features-for-much-less-Costs$_c$ has been traditionally considered the relative value of goods from various developing Asian countries, although this perception is changing as these countries develop.

The concept of relative value is less relevant to the pricing process and has little bearing on it.

2.5 Value-for-Money Concept

The *Value-for-money* concept is the mental way customers compare the amount of money they pay for a product to the quality they receive in the product.

Table 2.1 Value-for-money concept

Value-for-money concept	Higher price	Lower price
Higher value	Premium brand	Good deal
Lower value	Overcharging	Low-end

In this individual psychological process, customers view a connection between price and quality. Many customers maintain that products commanding a higher price are also of higher quality. This is a very common perception of how price and value interact in the mind of the customer.

Value is only relevant in the eyes of the beholder. This is why discounting a product can be extremely problematic, as it immediately devalues that product (Table 2.1).

2.6 Sales Axioms

The product's *Sales Axioms* are the fundamental concepts which the product is built upon.

Sales axioms serve to create an understanding on the reasons for a product's existence in the way that it is formed. The sales axioms identify and explain the fundamental concepts that are, in essence, the most basic traits the product provides.

Often, a product has between one and three sales axioms. That mix, or combination, of sales axioms at different degrees represents value to customers. The combination of sales axioms can also define and represent a product category.

For example, a consumer desktop operating system for personal computers, such as Microsoft Windows or Apple OS, might have the following sales axioms: simplicity (ease of use), maintainability (ease of maintenance), and productivity (scope of useful features).

Two to three sales axioms per product is considered to be sufficient. This is because people can easily comprehend two sales axioms (two-dimensional) on a virtual map. Three sales axioms (three-dimensional) on a virtual map are harder to intuitively grasp, but still possible. Most people cannot comprehend four or more sales axioms on a virtual map.

Use only factual, tangible, measurable attributes or features of a product as sales axioms. For example, for many midsized family cars, you might determine reliability, efficiency, and ease of service as the sales axioms. These are all factual and measurable.

Do not use an interpretation or subjective perception of the product's attributes or features. For example, intangible and immeasurable concepts such as status, prestige, style, quality, design, and beauty are not sales axioms.

Some products have a single dominant sales axiom that establishes the product's identity and dramatically influences that brand. For example, crashworthiness is a major sales axiom for Volvo cars. Reliability is a much-touted sales axiom for Toyota cars.

Many companies attempt to differentiate a product by adding another distinctive sales axiom that makes their product unique and more competitive in the market. Sometimes, this results in a product that is at the top of its current product category or a product that is alone in a new product category—*in a league of its own.*

2.7 Value Concept Retention Drill

1. What is the value formula?

   (a) Value = Features − $Costs_c$
   (b) Value = Benefits − TCO
   (c) Value = Features − TCO
   (d) Value = Benefits − $Costs_c$

2. What is value?

   (a) Usefulness or importance that the product holds for the customer
   (b) Benefits that something is held to deserve for a customer
   (c) Worth derived by the customer from owning and using the product
   (d) Monetary, material or assessed advantage of an asset, good or service

3. What is relative value?

   (a) A concept that addresses the ratio between benefits and $Costs_c$ that a product holds for customers
   (b) The implicit promise a product holds for customers to deliver a better ratio of gains relative to cost
   (c) A product's value that takes into account the value of similar products
   (d) The attractiveness of an investment in a product in comparison to another

4. What is a sales axiom?

   (a) The level of subjective usefulness or importance that the product holds for the customer
   (b) Direct financial gains by selling
   (c) A term used to identify and explain the fundamental concepts that the product is built upon
   (d) A pricing principle that is universally accepted within a practice or subject

Answers: 1-(d), 2-(c), 3-(b), 4-(c)

Chapter 3
Pricing Influencers

3.1 Introduction

This section contains key concepts and ideas that influence the pricing process through market and customer considerations.

3.2 Price-Based Competition

There is often a dominant factor, usually the product's price or feature set, that heavily influences potential customers to buy or reject a product. This main influencer is referred to as the *Buying Decision Factor*.

Sellers often emphasize price or value as the main buying decision factor. Less commonly, they emphasize features.

In *Price-based Competition*, the seller emphasizes price, whether high or low, as the main buying decision factor.

In *Value-based Competition*, the seller emphasizes value (convenience, features, quality, loyalty, delivery, etc.) as the main buying decision factor. Value-based competition also attempts to de-emphasize price as the buying decision factor.

Many businesses use variations of the "We are the cheapest" phrase to signal that they employ price-based competition, while other businesses portray themselves as "We are the best", hinting that they engage in value-based competition.

Feature-based Competition is an atypical form of competition that is reserved for luxury items and premium products (e.g. Rolex watches and Bugatti cars). In feature-based competition, the seller emphasizes the product's capabilities and characteristics as the main buying decision factor while de-emphasizing price and any other consideration.

G. Steinhardt, *Market-Value Pricing*, SpringerBriefs in Business,
https://doi.org/10.1007/978-3-030-10734-5_3

3.3 Price Wars

Formally, *Price Wars* are defined as continuous retaliatory price reductions to reach a price point that drives competitors out of the market.

Price wars are ultimately harmful to all warring parties because price wars imply or are caused by no product differentiation among competing products. Price wars suggest that competing products are commodities, which is a problematic situation for all vendors to compete in.

Commodities are defined as common products that have relatively the same feature set and no differentiators. Over time, the price of commodities converges at a very narrow price point. For example, a pound of sugar and Internet connectivity are common commodities nowadays.

Price wars are sometimes associated with dumping, a type of predatory pricing. *Dumping* is the selling of large quantities of goods at low prices, sometimes below cost and for an extended period of time. This is an intentional tactic to drive competition out of the market.

When specifically dealing in international markets, *Dumping* refers to the practice of companies selling their products in export markets at a price that is lower than the price they charge for their own products in their home markets.

Reasons companies engage in price wars include:

- There are no product differentiators.
- Buyers are unaware of any product differentiators.
- Companies have surpluses and over-capacity in manufacturing.
- Customers find it easy and inexpensive to switch to the competition.
- Vendors believe that frequent price reductions will drive market demand.
- Current economic conditions are bad, which elevates price sensitivity in the market.

You should avoid price wars due to their negative implications, but there are two justifiable conditions for initiating price reductions: when the company has a manufacturing, cost, or technological advantage over the competitors, or when overall demand for the product category will grow when you lower prices.

When pricing your product, assume that your competitors and buyers are well informed, and then strongly consider the competitors' and buyers' respective reactions to any price changes.

In general, you can lower prices to improve market share, increase unit sales, and raise profit, but do so without initiating price wars with the competition's efforts (Fig. 3.1).

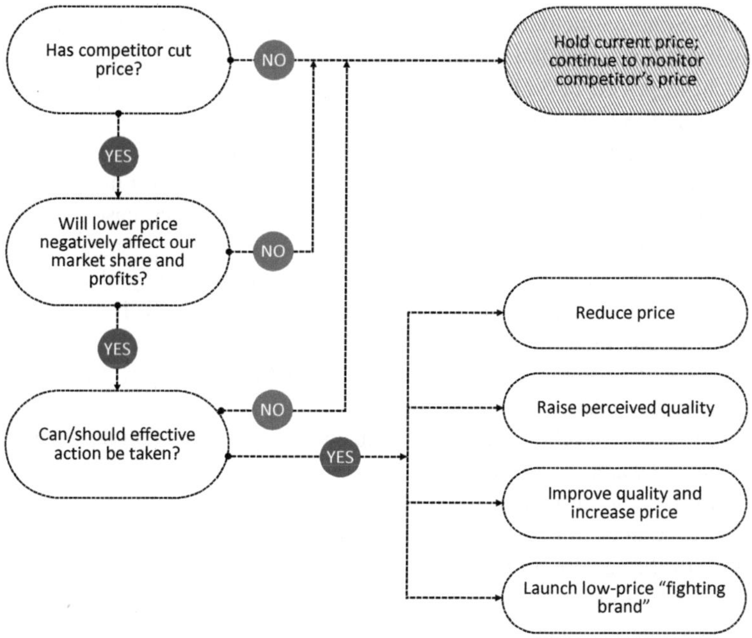

Fig. 3.1 Pricing wars decision support chart

3.4 Price Psychology

Price implicitly communicates information by giving customers a perception of the quality that they will receive from a given price for a product. This means that customers can interpret price levels in many ways: "hidden-catch", premium, leadership, low quality, high quality, economy model, "going-out-of-business", etc.

When you attempt to make sense of how people interpret prices, you employ *Price Psychology*. Price psychology describes a dynamic human reasoning process by which people infer diverse messages about the product and company. These inferences are based on the product's price, price comparisons, and price changes. Price psychology is a strong driving force that influences buying decisions.

Price affects the perception of quality—the customer's perceptions of prestige. Price can be an indicator of value. For example, TAG Heuer, the Swiss watchmaker, was in difficulties, and sales were low. In response, TAG Heuer raised the average price of its watches from $250 to $1000 without changing the products themselves. Consequently, TAG Heuer's sales volume increased sevenfold.

Buyers often want lower and upper price limits as a frame of reference for their buying decisions. Buyers perceive price changes in proportional terms, rather than absolute terms, and they believe that mid-range prices are a good compromise.

Williams-Sonoma is an American consumer retail company that sells high-end kitchenware and is headquartered in San Francisco, California. The company has successfully used lower and upper price limits to drive sales.

Williams-Sonoma included a mid-range bread machine in its product catalog for $279, but it did not sell well. In order to drive sales, Williams-Sonoma added a larger bread machine priced at $429 to its product catalog. Afterwards, the sales of the smaller machine ($279) almost doubled.

When changing product prices, research has shown that a series of small price increases below some upper threshold is more successful than one large increase. Contrarily, buyers favorably respond more to one large price decrease than to a series of small, successive price decreases.

Research has also shown that price arrangement, or the display of a list of several related product prices, has a direct impact on a buying decision. Product prices can be shown in ascending or descending order. When buyers are shown the higher price first, they are willing to pay more. When you show buyers the lower price first, they are inclined to pay less.

Another tactic to psychologically influence the buying decision through cosmetic presentation is *Odd/Even Pricing*. In this tactic, the price ends with certain digits, often the digit 9, to influence buyers' perceptions of the price or product. This practice is very common in the United States, where products are priced minus one cent, with the resulting price being, for example, $9.99.

Studies have found that odd/even pricing has some impact on buyers in the United States, but no impact was found in Western European countries. Odd pricing may signal a bargain, which may not be compatible with the desired image.

Before pricing, analyze the market and be aware that the industry's and the market's reactions to interpretations of price changes may vary considerably from what you expect.

3.5 Market Equilibrium

The economic theory of supply and demand asserts two things: suppliers are willing to produce more of a product if the price of the product increases, and customers are willing to buy more of a product if the price decreases.

Supply is the quantities of a product that will be offered to the market by suppliers at various prices. Conversely, *Demand* refers to the quantities of a product that will be bought in the market at various prices.

In lay terms, if supply increases, then the price will go down, or vice versa. If demand increases, then then price will go up, or vice versa.

When the market forces of supply and demand converge at a specific price point where supply meets demand and remains there, you have *Market Equilibrium*. Therefore, according to this economic theory, the market price of a product is a reflection of the present levels of supply and demand (Fig. 3.2).

Note that estimating demand curves is a retroactive and difficult process, and not applicable to new products.

Behavior of supply and demand is subject to *Price Elasticity*, which is the percentage change in quantity supplied or demanded that occurs in response to a

Fig. 3.2 Supply and demand

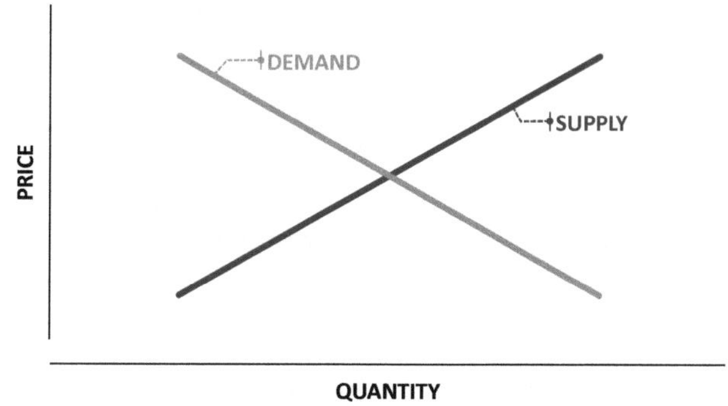

percentage change in price. Price elasticity is also known as price sensitivity. Most often, the focus is on price elasticity of demand.

Inelastic Demand exists when changes in the price do not significantly affect the quantity that is demanded by the market. This is opposed to *Elastic Demand*, which occurs when changes in price greatly affect the quantity that is demanded by the market.

The following factors affect price elasticity:

- *Information*—availability of factual market data
- *Comparisons*—ease of comparing products
- *Substitutes*—existence of alternatives
- *Switching*—changing products (cost, learning)

Certain market characteristics greatly affect price sensitivity. Higher price sensitivity occurs when there is awareness of substitutes and when substitutes are easily compared. A distinctive product, coupled with a high cost of switching between competing products, results in lower price sensitivity.

A premium demand curve presents a rather unique market situation where an increase in price meets with an increase in the quantity demanded by the market. This often occurs with luxury items, such as a country club membership, where demand increases as the price goes up.

An example of premium demand and how price can affect the customers' perception of quality and value is that of the dBase II software package.

Wayne Ratliff was a programmer at Jet Propulsion Laboratories in California during the late 1970s. Ratliff wrote a small database management program to manage a football lottery at the office, and he named the program Vulcan (after the home planet of Mr Spock, a character in the 1960s Star Trek TV series).

Ratliff himself unsuccessfully marketed Vulcan at $60 via mail order in 1979–1980. In late 1980, Ratliff met George Tate. Tate owned Ashton-Tate, a software marketing company (supposedly named after his parrot, Ashton). Ratliff and Ashton-Tate signed a marketing agreement for Ashton-Tate to market, sell, and distribute Vulcan.

George Tate renamed the Vulcan product dBASE, upped the version number to II because of a belief that the first version of a product would not sell well, and raised the price from $60 to $695.

dBase II became an immensely profitable product, paving the way to an even more profitable and hugely successful dBase III. Ashton-Tate was, during the early 1980s, one of the big three leading and wealthy software companies in the United States, which also included Microsoft and Lotus.

3.6 Business and Consumer Markets

Generally, the principles of pricing are universal and equally applicable to all types of business and consumer products.

There are, however, major differences between Business-to-Business (B2B) and Business-to-Consumer (B2C) markets. These differences are rooted in the nature of the engagement and the specific characteristics of the market.

In a B2B scenario, demand is influenced by other markets, there are a few customers with large budgets, there are professional buyers and sellers who make rational decisions, there is a lengthy negotiation process, and once a deal is struck, the vendor and the customer hope for a long-term relationship.

In a B2C scenario, demand is intrinsically created, there are many customers with limited budgets, the buyers and sellers are untrained and often make emotional decisions, there is a short negotiation process, and once a deal is struck, there is very little loyalty between the vendor and the customer (Table 3.1).

3.7 Product Life Cycle Model

The *Product Life Cycle Model* (PLC model) is a theory which identifies the distinct stages affecting sales of a product, from the product's inception until its retirement.

At the core of the PLC model are the assumptions that all products have limited life spans and that the product sales pass through different and distinct stages.

Table 3.1 B2B versus B2C characteristics

Business-to-Business (B2B)	Business-to-Consumer (B2C)
Other markets influence demand	Demand is intrinsically created
Few customers	Many customers
Customers with large budgets	Customers with limited budgets
Professional buyers and sellers who make rational decisions	Untrained buyers and sellers who often make emotional decisions
Lengthy negotiation process	Short negotiation process
Hope for long-term relationship	Little loyalty

Fig. 3.3 Product life cycle model stages

Different products have different life cycles, and the shape of the PLC curve determines the revenue earned. Each stage in the PLC model requires different marketing and pricing strategies.

Marketers traditionally view a PLC as being comprised of four distinct stages: introduction, growth, maturity, and decline (Fig. 3.3).

In the *Introduction* stage, the product is introduced to the market through a focused and intense marketing effort designed to establish a clear identity and promote maximum awareness. Many trial or impulse purchases occur at this stage. Next, consumer interest brings about the *Growth* stage, distinguished by increasing sales and the emergence of competitors.

The growth stage is also characterized by sustaining marketing activities on the vendor's side, with consumers engaged in repeat purchase behavior patterns. The product reaches the *Maturity* stage when competitors begin to leave the market, sales velocity is dramatically reduced, and sales volume reaches a steady state. At this point in time, mostly loyal consumers purchase the product.

A continuous decline in sales signals entry into the *Decline* stage. The lingering effects of competition, unfavorable economic conditions, new fashion trends, etc. often explain the decline in sales.

The PLC model makes sense, but practically applying it is challenging because it is difficult to predict the overall cycle shape, the length of each stage, the product's stage transition, and to map the product's current stage location.

Use the product life cycle model to forecast sales performance and apply stage-dependent prices.

3.8 Pricing Influencers Retention Drill

1. Which is an atypical form of competition that is reserved for luxury items?

   (a) Price-based competition
   (b) Feature-based competition
   (c) Value-based competition
   (d) Product-based competition

2. Why are price wars a problematic situation for all vendors to compete in?

(a) Price wars suggest that competing products are commodities
(b) Price wars cause market stagnation
(c) Price wars de-emphasize price and any other consideration
(d) Price wars drive prices up

3. People infer diverse messages about the product and company based on the product's price. What is the name of this process?

   (a) Price analytics
   (b) Price inferences
   (c) Price psychology
   (d) Price reasoning

4. Which condition is needed for market equilibrium to occur?

   (a) Supply and demand converge at a specific price point and remain there
   (b) Awareness of substitutes is high, and substitutes are easily compared
   (c) The percentage change in quantity supplied or demanded is identical
   (d) The price does not affect the quantity that is demanded by the market

5. Which are characteristics of a Business-to-Business (B2B) market? (multiple response)

   (a) Lengthy negotiation process
   (b) Little loyalty
   (c) Few customers
   (d) Limited budgets

6. Which *Product Life Cycle Model* (PLC model) stage is characterized by diminishing sales?

   (a) Introduction
   (b) Growth
   (c) Maturity
   (d) Decline

Answers: 1-(b), 2-(a), 3-(c), 4-(a), 5-(a, c), 6-(d)

Chapter 4
MVP Model

4.1 Introduction

This section introduces the *Blackblot Market-Value Pricing™ Model* (MVP Model), a market-value centric pricing process. This process guides sets of managerial decisions that help determine a product's price.

4.2 Basic Pricing Knowledge Elements

You should establish several essential knowledge prerequisites before putting the MVP Model to use.

At the most basic level, you should have data, or at least a good understanding of the following:

- Costs associated with the product
- The level of demand presented by the market
- The level and type of value that the customer will attribute to the product
- The price of substitutes and competing products
- Familiarity with political, social, legal, and economic environments

The *Total Costs* associated with the product are the sum of costs of goods, selling costs, and overhead costs (fixed or variable) (Fig. 4.1).

The *Costs of Goods* include all manufacturing, material, and labor costs. *Selling Costs* are all costs directly related to selling. *Overhead Costs* are any non-direct costs, such as marketing, salaries, storage, or interest paid.

Fixed Costs include any cost that remains constant as the quantity produced or sold varies. *Variable Costs* are costs that vary with the quantity produced or sold.

G. Steinhardt, *Market-Value Pricing*, SpringerBriefs in Business,
https://doi.org/10.1007/978-3-030-10734-5_4

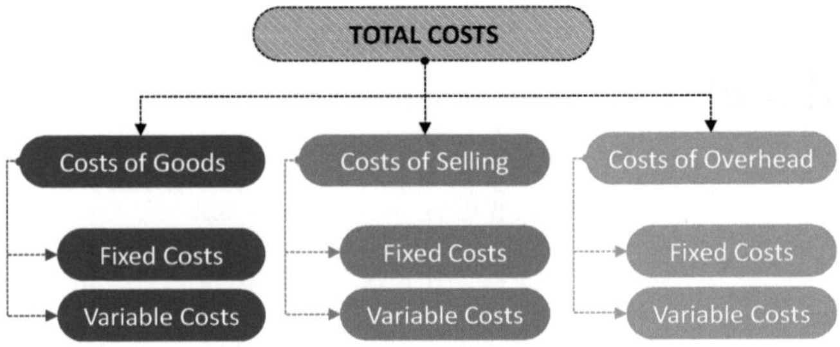

Fig. 4.1 Total costs

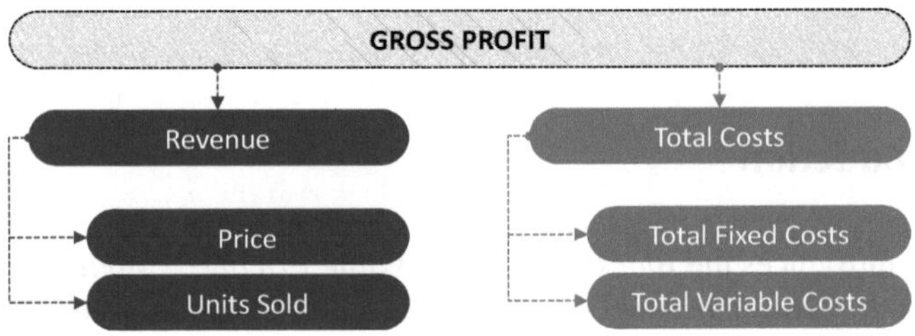

Fig. 4.2 Gross profit elements

4.3 Gross Profit Formula

Gross Profit is the financial gain, before taxes, from selling products. Calculate the gross profit by subtracting the total costs from the total revenue. *Total Revenue* is the monies received from selling a product. To determine total revenue, multiply the price of the product by the quantity of units sold (Fig. 4.2).

Use the following simplified formula to figure the gross profit:

$$\text{Gross Profit} = \text{Total Revenue} - \text{Total Costs}$$

The internal elements of the gross profit formula are interrelated. For example, modifying the price may affect both the quantity of units sold and the total variable costs.

4.4 Blackblot Market-Value Pricing™ Model

Developed by Blackblot®—Product Management Expertise™, the *Blackblot Market-Value Pricing*™ Model (MVP Model) is comprised of three distinct components. These components effectively act as sequential stages in the pricing process: pricing scheme, pricing formula, and price mix (Fig. 4.3).

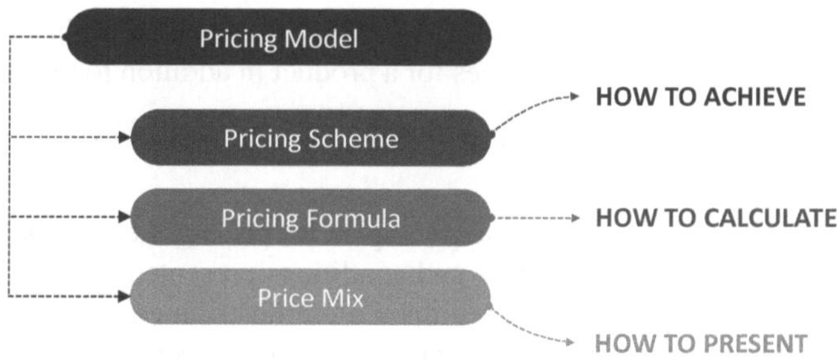

Fig. 4.3 MVP model components

The MVP Model's *Pricing Scheme* provides an outline of the overall pricing approach, which encompasses the principles for pricing the specific product. The pricing scheme is focused on how to achieve the desired pricing objectives.

The MVP Model's *Pricing Formula* is a calculatory structure that allows you to apply pricing changes to specific markets or competitive regions. The pricing formula is focused on how to amend the price based on specific conditions and needs.

The MVP Model's *Price Mix* is a price-related aggregate of information and conditions that the customer is presented with. The price mix is focused on how to present the price and its additions to the customer.

The MVP Model presents a sequential pricing process with the following phases:

1. Secure knowledge prerequisites
2. Determine pricing objectives
3. Select pricing strategy
4. Choose life cycle stage pricing tactics
5. Devise a pricing formula
6. Assemble a price mix

4.5 MVP Model Retention Drill

1. Which are the three major components of the MVP Model?

   (a) Price Scheme, Price Structure, Price Blend
   (b) Pricing Strategy, Pricing Tactics, Price Mix
   (c) Pricing Formula, Pricing Goals, Price Merge
   (d) Pricing Scheme, Pricing Formula, Price Mix

2. What is the objective and description of the Pricing Scheme component of the MVP Model?

   (a) Overall pricing approach of the principles for pricing the specific product
   (b) Calculatory structure that allows pricing changes to specific markets

(c) Aggregate of price information and conditions presented to the customer
(d) Setting a range of standard prices for a product in addition to the default price

3. What is the objective and description of the Pricing Formula component of the MVP Model?

(a) Overall pricing approach of the principles for pricing the specific product
(b) Aggregate of price information and conditions presented to the customer
(c) Arrangement to sell that is based upon a pre-determined calculation
(d) Calculatory structure that allows pricing changes to specific markets

4. What is the objective and description of the Price Mix component of the MVP Model?

(a) Overall pricing approach of the principles for pricing the specific product
(b) Aggregate of price information and conditions presented to the customer
(c) Calculatory structure that allows pricing changes to specific markets
(d) Worth of the product as determined by the manufacturer, not the customer

Answers: 1-(d), 2-(a), 3-(d), 4-(b)

4.6 MVP Model

The MVP Model is a market-value centric pricing process which guides you through sets of managerial decisions, helping you determine a product's price. The MVP Model is comprised of three distinct components that effectively act as sequential stages in the pricing process: *Pricing Scheme, Pricing Formula*, and *Price Mix* (Fig. 4.4).

The MVP Model embodies a market-value pricing concept that is as structured as possible, yet you must always keep in mind that price setting is full of contradictions and trade-offs.

4.7 Pricing Scheme

The pricing scheme is comprised of three components, which you should execute sequentially. In essence, each component is a junction at which you make decisions.

The first decision junction is *Objectives*. In Objectives, you describe what a company wants to achieve through pricing its products.

The second decision junction is *Strategies*. This is a primary method of pricing that relies on a particular pricing decision factor.

The third decision junction is *Tactics*. Tactics are pricing actions which are dependent on the particular life cycle stage of the product that is being priced.

The following sections describe the pricing scheme components in more detail.

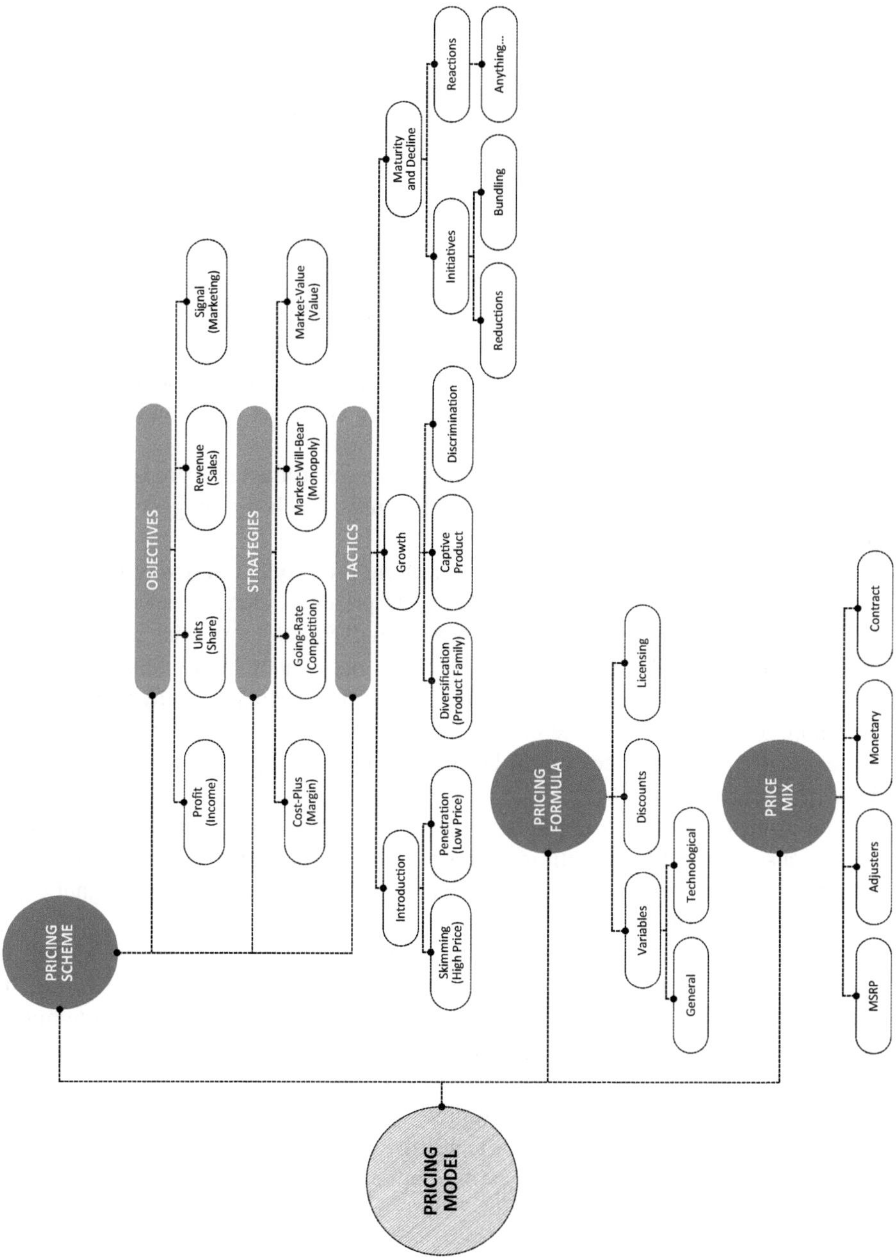

Fig. 4.4 MVP model

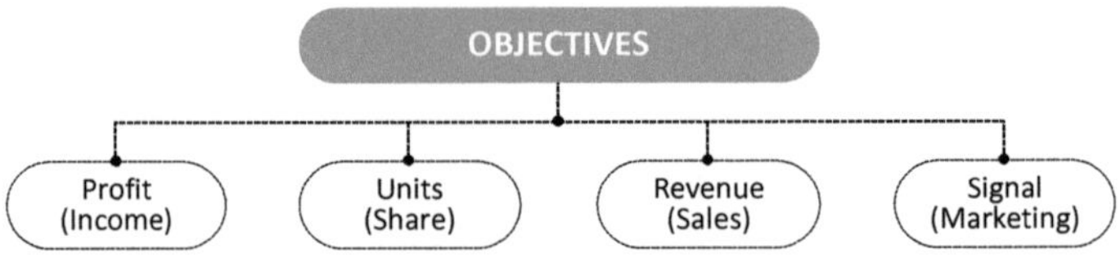

Fig. 4.5 MVP model pricing objectives

4.8 Pricing Objectives

A business hopes to achieve one or more of four different types of pricing objectives through the act of pricing (Fig. 4.5).

The *Profit* pricing objective is the most common, as the product's price helps to attain the most financial gain. This means that the product's price helps make as much profit (the difference between monies earned and monies expended) as possible. Depending on the market situation, the company may obtain a profit by pricing the products relatively low or relatively high.

The *Units* pricing objective means that pricing the product is geared to help sell as many product units as possible and, consequently, reach the biggest market share possible.

The *Revenue* pricing objective means pricing the product in a way that leads to the largest volume of sales. The business sets prices to increase revenue (product price multiplied by units sold), which is essentially the total monies received from selling the product. Maximum revenue does not necessarily imply maximum profit.

The *Signaling* pricing objective means pricing the product in a way that indicates the nature of the product, or the intentions of the business, to the market or industry. For example, product prices might be reduced temporarily to create excitement or draw more customers.

You can use the *Signaling* pricing objective to signal a range of ideas and intents to both customers and competitors. These include *Class*, where the unusually high price indicates a premium brand. Price is an especially important quality signal when customers are unable to judge the product's quality.

Drastically lowering prices may indicate one of three stances to the market. In *Survival* mode, the company is just trying to stay afloat by only covering its operating costs. An *Aggressive* stance means the business makes an attempt to initiate a price war. In a *Defensive* position, the business lowers prices to intimidate potential market entrants.

When a business does not modify prices in the face of a fluctuating market in turmoil, this may indicate *Stability*. Here, the business keeps prices steady, particularly from declining, in order to avoid a price war.

4.9 Pricing Objectives Clarifications

Different price levels can achieve different pricing objectives while maintaining a consistent cost structure. Businesses must choose the appropriate pricing objective that supports their agenda.

For example, Apple's pricing objective is to attain as much profit as possible, since there is reportedly a 50% margin on the price of Apple computers. Contrarily, Hewlett-Packard subsidizes the price of their Inkjet and LaserJet printers. This implies that Hewlett-Packard applies the Units pricing objective, which seeks the biggest market share in printers. Hewlett-Packard then makes its money from the sale of printer ink and toner, which implies the Profit pricing objective for these consumables.

Sony applies the Signaling pricing objective. Sony commonly tries to be the most expensive offering in the category and thus attempts to create a class association—an indication to the market that they are a premium brand.

Microsoft, on the other hand, does not recoil from using the Signaling pricing objective to communicate that their products are cheaper. Microsoft does this particularly when it comes to consumer products such as the Xbox game console and Microsoft Surface tablets, whose marketplace performance does not adversely impact Microsoft's brand value and core business of desktop operating systems.

Deciding upon and selecting a particular pricing objective is dependent on many factors. A certain pricing objective may be relevant or irrelevant at different times and conditions. Accordingly, you can sequence and alternate pricing objectives, often according to a product's current life cycle stage.

While profit maximization is generally the priority at many businesses, it may not ultimately be a valid choice. This is because your selected pricing objective must support the business strategy and be consistent with the market strategy.

There is no one apparent pricing objective for a specific set of market conditions. In addition, no particular price level can help achieve a pricing objective. For example, the profit pricing objective does not specify or mandate a certain price level—it can either be a high or low price strategy.

In the context of the MVP Model, you select any pricing objective only to establish a cognitive backdrop to future pricing decisions. There are no direct calculations in the MVP Model that hinge upon pricing objectives.

4.10 Pricing Strategies

Pricing Strategies describe the primary available pricing methods that a business can select from and use to determine a price. Each of the specific methods relies on a particular pricing decision factor.

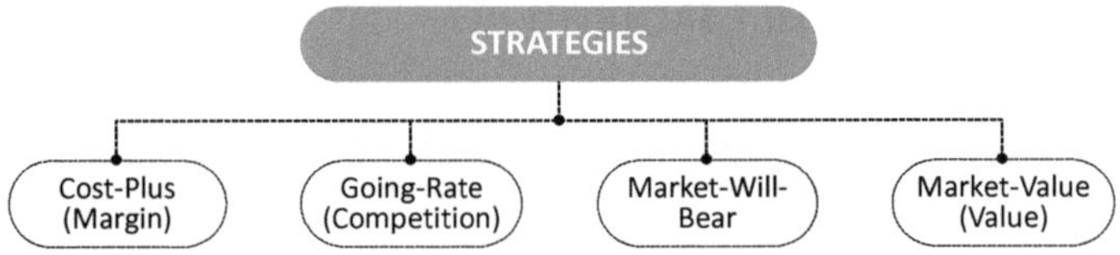

Fig. 4.6 MVP model pricing strategies

The MVP Model presents four possible pricing strategies that are available as part of the MVP Model's pricing scheme: cost-plus, going-rate, market-will-bear, and market-value (Fig. 4.6).

4.11 Cost-Plus Pricing Strategy

The *Cost-plus* pricing strategy, also referred to as cost-based pricing, is a simple method of pricing in which a specified nominal or percentile amount, known as the margin, is added to the unit cost of production of an item to determine its selling price.

Cost-plus pricing is wholly internally focused on the business, ignoring the customer and the market. This pricing approach inherently creates a mismatch between the price and the customer. The cost-plus pricing strategy uses the costs of producing the product as the primary decision factor in determining the product's price.

Approximately 70% of businesses in the United States use the cost-based pricing strategy. Businesses cite the main reasons for doing cost-plus pricing as its ease, difficulty in estimating customer value, and difficulty in assessing the market demand function.

The *Going-rate* pricing strategy is also referred to as competition-oriented, competition-based, or reference-based pricing strategy. In this pricing method, the business determines the price of the product more by the price of a similar product sold by a powerful competitor than by considerations of market demand and cost of production.

The going-rate pricing strategy uses competitors' prices as the primary pricing decision factor in determining the product's price and is often found in markets which are dominated by one vendor.

For example, Cisco is a globally dominant United States-based company which deals in networking and telecommunications equipment. *Cisco-pricing* is a colloquial reference to a manner of pricing where a network equipment vendor prices its own products by referencing the price of Cisco's competing product.

When applying the going-rate pricing strategy, the business doing the pricing analyzes the dominant competitor's costs, prices, quality of offering, and possible reactions to having competitors pricing their products similarly. Businesses expect competitor reactions when competing products from different vendors are perceived to be similar, buyers are well informed, and there are few competitors in the market. The current estimate is that about 40% of technology companies use the going-rate pricing strategy.

The going-rate pricing strategy is a bit more complex than cost-plus pricing and also somewhat detached from the business's customers. The cost-plus and going-rate pricing strategies are simple and easy to implement but ignore market dynamics, price sensitivity, and demand functions. Value is the last derived factor when using cost-based and going-rate pricing strategies.

In addition, a major fault with the going-rate pricing strategy is that it ignores the competitor's market success or failure.

4.12 Market-Will-Bear Pricing Strategy

The *Market-will-bear* pricing strategy, also referred to as target-pricing or monopoly-pricing, is an attempt at charging the highest possible price without running into harsh negative consequences. An estimated 8% of technology companies attempt to use market-will-bear pricing.

The market-will-bear pricing strategy uses unfair competitive advantages and market dependencies as the primary decision factor in determining the product's price.

For example, OPEC (Organization of Petroleum Exporting Countries) attempts to manipulate and maintain a high price for oil, mainly through limiting supply via production quotas. In addition, electric companies, the pharmaceutical industry, financial and banking services, and even governments, all border on the market-will-bear pricing strategy.

A short-term type of the market-will-bear pricing strategy is *Price Gouging*. Price gouging, a felony in the United States, is the legal term for excessively charging for essentials (such as drinking water) during civil emergencies. Price gouging is a unique occurrence that is characterized by vendors who are willing to supply their product at an excessive price rather than compete with each other by lowering the price of their products. The only remedy to price gouging is governmental regulation.

Another notable felony in the United States is *Price Fixing*. In price fixing, two or more parties conspire to sell their competing product at a set price. Price fixing is wrong because it establishes a barrier to entry, impeding innovation, slowing economic growth, and reducing quality of living by overcharging consumers.

4.13 Market-Value Pricing Strategy

The *Market-value* pricing strategy relies on customers' relative importance and paying tendency as the primary pricing decision factor. The Market-value pricing strategy is also referred as a value-based, value-driven, market-driven, or value pricing strategy.

There are three methods to determine the market-value price of a product: declared price, inferred price, and derived price.

The *Declared Price* method is an explicit approach where customers are interviewed and literally asked how much money they are willing to pay for the product. In this instance, the customer formally declares the price which they are willing to pay for the product. Yet it is rather obvious that the customer is aware of or suspects what is being done, and therefore skews the declared price downwards.

The *Inferred Price* method is an implicit approach where customers are interviewed and literally asked how important, useful, beneficial, etc. that product is to them relative to another substitute, alternative, or competing product of which the price is known. The business then concludes the price of the product through judging the customers' answers.

For example, a brand of mineral water is being priced via the inferred price method and customers are asked to rate the mineral water on a scale with carbonated soft drinks and fruit juices. The commercial market prices of the carbonated soft drinks and fruit juices are known. If the mineral water is rated similarly to fruit juices, then the deduced assumption is that mineral water should be priced similarly to the fruit juices.

The *Derived Price* method is a structured approach where customers provide an indication of the level of attributed benefit/s the product provides. The price of the product is then calculated in accordance to the level of the attributed benefit/s.

For example, customers are asked to try a new chair design and indicate how comfortable the chair is to sit on. The business then quantifies and monetizes the level of comfort that the chair provides, a major attributed benefit for a chair, in addition to other possible attributed benefits, such as adjustability and general ergonomics. Thus, the chair's price is determined.

With the derived price method, you use either of two techniques—whole offering and sales axiom factors—to determine the attributed benefit and then reach a derived price. [Note: for a detailed explanation on the concept of sales axioms, please refer to *Sales Axioms* in the *Value Concept* section].

All the market-value pricing strategy methods (declared price, inferred price, and derived price) focus on the customers' perception of value, not on cost or the competition's price, in order to make a pricing decision.

Therefore, your starting point for any of the market-value pricing strategy methods (particularly the derived price method) is in truly understanding the customer.

4.14 Derived Price: Whole Offering Technique

The derived price method deserves more consideration and detail, as there are two techniques to determine the attributed benefit to reach a derived price: whole offering and sales axiom factors.

With the *Whole Offering* technique, customers rate and compare the relative quality of each product separately as one complete unit. For example, customers view several automobiles and rate each vehicle separately as a complete unit that represents a combination of features and benefits. The product manager then quantifies and monetizes the score rating given to each vehicle, thus determining the derived price.

The whole offering technique is based on a benefit score, which is given to the whole product. The score, totaling 100 points, is allocated to all products being compared.

The idea of an *Attributed Benefit Formula* was originally conceived at the University of Chicago Graduate School of Business. Later, Blackblot fully developed the formula and concept.

Use the attributed benefit formula to calculate the attributed benefit in the whole offering method (Fig. 4.7).

For example, an umbrella manufacturer wants to select the best price for its product ("Winter Umbrella"). The main rival is another company's umbrella ("Storm Umbrella"). Assume a survey with a sufficient sample discovers that, on average, customers allocate 60 points to Winter Umbrella and 40 points to Storm Umbrella. The hypothetical official market price of Storm Umbrella is $10.

With these parameters, you can complete the attributed benefit formula in the whole offering method, and then try a range of prices for Winter Umbrella. From the range of prices, you can then select a specific price. If you hypothetically give Winter Umbrella a price of $12, then the calculated benefit and the resulting value is positive and higher than that of Storm Umbrella. This means that a price of $12 for Winter Umbrella is a viable option (Table 4.1).

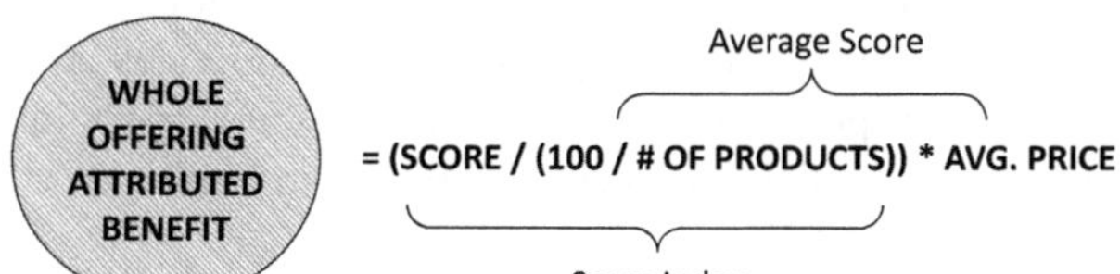

Fig. 4.7 Whole offering attributed benefit formula

Table 4.1 Example of whole offering technique

Product	Score	Price	Derived benefit	Value
Winter Umbrella	60_{pts}	$12	$13.2	+$1.2
Storm Umbrella	40_{pts}	$10	$8.8	−$1.2

- Benefit = (Score/(100pts/# of Products)) × Avg. Price
- Derived Benefit Winter Umbrella = (60pts/(100pts/2)) × $11 = $13.2
- Derived Benefit Storm Umbrella = (40pts/(100pts/2)) × $11 = $8.8

4.15 Derived Price: Sales Axioms Factors Technique

With the *Sales Axioms Factors* technique, customers rate and compare the relative quality of several products' weighted sales axioms.

For example, many customers consider reliability (minimal malfunctions), fuel efficiency, and serviceability (ease of maintenance)—in this particular order—as the most important sales axioms in a passenger vehicle. Customers judge several automobiles and separately score the level of each of the sales axioms that each vehicle provides. The product manager then quantifies and monetizes the aggregate weighted score given to each vehicle's sales axioms. Thus, the derived price is determined.

You can also use a variation of the attributed benefit formula to calculate the attributed benefit in the sales axiom factors method. First, generate a score index using a weighted benefit score given to each of the sales axioms. Then, calculate the sales axioms' attributed benefit by multiplying the score index by the average price (Fig. 4.8).

As for the hypothetical example of pricing an umbrella using the sales axioms factors technique, there could be several different sales axioms related to an umbrella. For simplicity in this example, assume that the sales axioms for an umbrella are ostensibly durability (ability to withstand the rigors of nature) and coverage (scope of protecting against water).

Assume that a survey with a sufficient sample discovers that, on average, customers allocate 55 points for durability and 45 points for coverage. For the sales axiom of durability, customers also allocate 75 points to Winter Umbrella and 25 points to Storm Umbrella. For the sales axiom of coverage, customers allocate 55 points to Winter Umbrella and 45 points to Storm Umbrella. The hypothetical official market price of Storm Umbrella is $10.

- **Score Index** = [(SalesAxiom#1 Score / (100_{pts} / # of Products)) • SalesAxiom#1Weight] + [(SalesAxiom#2 Score / (100_{pts} / # of Products)) • SalesAxiom#2Weight] + [(SalesAxiom#n Score / (100_{pts} / # of Products)) • SalesAxiom#1nWeight]
- **Sales Axioms Factors Attributed Benefit** = Score Index • Avg. Price

Fig. 4.8 Sales axioms factors attributed benefit formula

Table 4.2 Example of sales axioms factors technique

Product	Durability	Coverage	Value	Benefits	Price
Winter Umbrella	75 points	55 points	$4.19	$11.19	$7.00
Storm Umbrella	25 points	45 points	−$4.19	$5.81	$10.00
Sales Axiom Weight	55%	45%	100%		

With these parameters, you can complete the attributed benefit formula in the sales axioms factors method, trying a range of prices for Winter Umbrella, and then select a specific price from these. If, hypothetically, you give Winter Umbrella a price of $7, then the calculated benefit and the resulting value are still positive and higher than that of Storm Umbrella (Table 4.2).

4.16 Base Price

Whether you select the cost-plus, going-rate, market-will-bear, or market-value pricing strategy, you need to use the resulting number as input and as the starting price in the next stage in the MVP Model, the pricing tactics.

This starting price is the *Base Price*, which means the initial price of a product before any alteration. Use the selected pricing strategy to determine the base price.

4.17 Pricing Strategies Retention Drill

1. Which is a pricing strategy that uses unfair competitive advantages and market dependencies?

   (a) Cost-plus
   (b) Going-rate
   (c) Market-value
   (d) Market-will-bear

2. Which pricing practices are considered to be a felony in the United States? (multiple response)

   (a) Price mending
   (b) Price gouging
   (c) Price alteration
   (d) Price fixing

3. Which is not a method that is used to determine the market-value price of a product?

   (a) Deduced price

(b) Declared price
(c) Inferred price
(d) Derived price

4. What is a Derived Price?

(a) Price that is declared by the customer
(b) Price that is concluded via customer surveys
(c) Price that is extrapolated from the production costs
(d) Price that is determined by attributed benefit

5. What is a Base Price?

(a) The initial price of a product before any alteration
(b) Price that is determined by attributed benefit
(c) A fixed price that enables limited time use of the product
(d) Fundamental cost of a product with any extra fees

Answers: 1-(d), 2-(b, d), 3-(a), 4-(d), 5-(a)

4.18 Pricing Tactics

Pricing Tactics are the pricing actions which are dependent on the particular life cycle stage of the product being priced.

The MVP Model presents seven possible pricing tactics as part of the MVP Model's pricing scheme, subject to a particular life cycle stage (Fig. 4.9):

- *Introduction Life Cycle Stage*—skimming or penetration pricing tactics
- *Growth Life Cycle Stage*—diversification, captive product, or discrimination pricing tactics
- *Maturity and Decline Life Cycle Stages*—initiatives or reactions pricing tactics

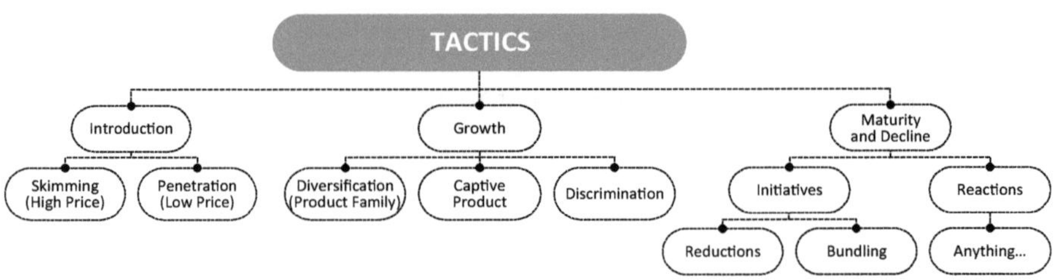

Fig. 4.9 MVP model pricing tactics

4.19 Introduction Life Cycle Stage

You can apply two types of pricing tactics to the base price in the introduction life cycle stage: the skimming pricing tactic and the penetration pricing tactic.

With the *Skimming* pricing tactic, the business briefly charges a relatively high price upon product launch. The *Penetration* pricing tactic means that the business briefly charges a relatively low price upon product launch.

The assumption behind both skimming and penetration pricing tactics is that in any market, some people can pay more, and some people can only afford to pay less.

The logic for skimming is that setting a high price for a new product gains maximum revenues from segments willing to pay the high price. Similarly, the logic for penetration pricing is that setting a low price for a new product attracts a large number of buyers with limited budgets, which will ultimately pave the way to a large market share.

In the skimming pricing tactic, the business charges the highest possible price to sell to small but profitable segments, taking advantage of early adopters. Skimming works well with a new, innovative, or improved product, but its disadvantage is that it encourages new competitors or market entrants.

The penetration pricing tactic attempts to gain a large, if not dominant, market share and maximize revenue impact. Penetration works well and caters to low-price point segments and is designed to generate many trial purchases. Its disadvantage is the low-positioning status and devaluation of the product. Penetration pricing is a temporary tactic that capitalizes on lower segments before ultimately raising prices.

The penetration pricing tactic is based on the theory that an initial low price helps secure market acceptance and forms habits among customers. A special variant of the penetration pricing tactic is the practice of *Everyday Low Pricing* (EDLP). EDLP is a pricing tactic of continuously offering low prices rather than relying on short-term price cuts such as cents-off coupons, rebates, and special sales. Walmart, a United States-based chain of discount department stores and warehouse stores, has successfully utilized the EDLP tactic (Table 4.3).

An example of penetration pricing is that of Samsung, which sells its Galaxy range of smart phones, loaded with the Android operating system, at a considerably discounted price. The objective is to increase market share for after-sales service,

Table 4.3 Skimming and penetration pricing tactics

Skimming	Penetration
Briefly charging high prices at launch	Briefly charging low prices at launch
Gain maximum revenue from segments willing to pay higher prices	Attract large number of buyers with limited budgets
Take advantage of early adopters	Gain large market share and maximize revenue
Works with innovative products	Generates trial purchases
Encourages new competitors	Devalues product

capture first-time buyers, and promote habit formation and familiarity with the Galaxy phones. This, in turn, leads to repeat purchases, upgrades, and referrals.

A classic example of skimming is of Apple, which has consistently and successfully used this tactic with the iPhone, given the conditions of high customer loyalty and when the product is new and innovative.

Apple has traditionally used skimming when launching its products, and pre-availability interest for the iPhone is proof that price-skimming was appropriate. The very first iPhone, with 8 GB of memory, was introduced with a price of $599. Less than three months after the product's introduction, Apple reduced the iPhone's price to $399.

Apple introduced the iPhone at $599 to capitalize on the early adopters' tendency to hastily buy new technology. As initial demand subsided, Apple reduced the price to $399 in an attempt to revive demand. Apple sold at least 500,000 iPhones at $599, making $100 million in extra profit by exploiting favorable market conditions and cleverly using the skimming pricing tactic.

From this example, we can deduce that the base price for the first iPhone with 8 GB of memory was $399 all along, and that Apple temporarily placed a markup of $200 as a consequence of applying the skimming pricing tactic.

In general, and during the introduction life cycle stage, you should apply the penetration pricing tactic when the product has no significant differentiators or is considered a loss leader (a product sold at cost or below cost to encourage sales of other profitable products). Apply the skimming pricing tactic when the customers are affluent, the product is of high value, the company has market dominance, competition is minimal, and/or demand for the product is strong.

4.20 Growth Life Cycle Stage

You can apply one of three types of pricing tactics to the base price in the growth life cycle stage: diversification, captive product, and discrimination.

With the *Diversification* pricing tactic, the business creates product variants with distributed price points. A business uses *Captive Product* pricing by offering a heavily subsidized core product but charging high prices on any other product that works with or is necessary for the functioning of the core product. The *Discrimination* pricing tactic has the business selling an identical product at different prices in different markets.

The *Diversification* pricing tactic allows you to create a range of product variants and set price steps between them. Each variant offers more features and capabilities at a higher price.

In high-tech, particularly in software, it is common to see lite, standard, professional, and enterprise product variants. In consumer goods, the same basic principle remains. Equivalent terms are often economy, classic, and flagship product variants.

Businesses often refer to the price of the low-end variant as *Bait Price* and the high-end variant as *Premium Price*. Although the low-end variant is limited in some way or ways, companies hope that most customers buy the standard product version. The professional product is for high-end segments, yet at the same time it can make the standard version seem like a good deal.

With the *Captive Product* pricing tactic, a business creates an imbalanced price ratio between the product's components, which are sold separately. With this tactic, the main system component is underpriced and the consumables or support services are overpriced.

The captive product pricing tactic is evident when the product is under-equipped and stripped of any major features or functionality. The offering constitutes a plan to sell optional and accessory products along with the main product. Many automobile manufacturers extensively use this approach, where the basic vehicle is stripped of many features. Then, the manufacturer prices optional extras such as a navigation system, parking sensors, glass roof, heated seats, etc. separately and sometimes expensively.

Many companies use the captive product pricing tactic. For example, Gillette, a United States-based brand of safety razors and other shaving supplies, sells the holding handle for Gillette safety razors exceedingly cheaply, while the price for razor blade replacement cartridges is exceedingly high. Hewlett-Packard's popular Inkjet and LaserJet printers are sold at a heavily subsidized price that is markedly lower than the price of a replacement ink or toner cartridge. Panasonic's line of Lumix cameras can only be used with proprietary batteries, made by Panasonic, which only fit Lumix cameras. Apple's various Apple computer and smartphone accessories are proprietary and required for normal operations; these are only available from Apple and only work with Apple products.

The *Discrimination* pricing tactic dictates charging different market segments different prices for the same product. This pricing tactic works well in monopolistic markets where the market segments cannot resell the product to each other, and when the costs of segmenting and policing the market in the interest of discrimination do not exceed the extra revenue. In order for price discrimination to work, the market segments must also differ by their income levels and their paying tendency.

Universal Pricing is the opposite of price discrimination. With universal pricing, every customer is charged the exact same price for the product.

Price discrimination is considered unfair, arguably unethical, and causes resentment, but price discrimination is illegal only if the intent is to destroy competition. Price discrimination is legal if it does not lessen or attempt to lessen the competition. In addition, price discrimination is allowed if you can justify differences in prices to different segments by differences in costs incurred when selling to each of the different segments.

In the United States, under the Robinson–Patman Act, a manufacturer cannot engage in price discrimination if the intent is to lessen or prevent competition for customers. This applies to manufacturers not discriminating against their own customers, which are the retail stores. The Robinson–Patman Act relates to manufacturers and originally grew out of practices in which chain stores were allowed to purchase goods from manufacturers at lower prices than other retailers.

There are three different levels of price discrimination. *First Level Price Discrimination* occurs when the seller presents each customer with a different price that is based on and calculated according to that customer's economic ability to pay that specific price. This type of price discrimination is also called charge-per-income. Shippers practiced this type of price discrimination during the previous centuries in England. A customer who had goods to ship overseas indicated their level of wealth by presenting their bank statement. The shipper gave a price for shipping merchandise according to the customer's bank deposits.

Second Level Price Discrimination is applied when universal pricing is seemingly available. In reality, the seller employs a variety of artificial obstacles (targeted coupons, advance purchase, restricted use, payment terms, or discounts) to effectively modify the actual price each segment pays. For example, the airline industry does second level price discrimination (based on restricted use and advance purchase) which discriminates against the more affluent business travelers. The airline industry also does third level price discrimination (based on age) in favor of students and senior citizens, which again discriminates against the more affluent business travelers. This is put into practice where, for example, the only purpose that a Saturday night stay-over requirement on airfares serves is to make lower-priced fares unattractive to relatively less sensitive business travelers. These airfare conditions, which are not favorable for business travelers, serve as a means to enforce second level price discrimination.

Second level price discrimination is practiced by many businesses, such as florist shops, where the price is based on a special event. It discriminates against customers when they buy a flower bouquet for a wedding at a high price, as opposed to selling that very same flower bouquet at a lower price for any other occasion.

Although any type of price discrimination is considered unjust or prejudicial, second level price discrimination is the only form of price discrimination that is considered somewhat acceptable by the public.

Third Level Price Discrimination is a highly sensitive and possibly politically and culturally charged practice in which external factors (e.g. gender, age, race, geography, and profession) serve to favorably or adversely alter the price each customer or market segment is presented with. For example, financial aid provided at universities to members of groups such as racial minorities is essentially discriminatory and based on race. Academic pricing of software in which academic institutions receive major discounts as opposed to regular business is third level price discrimination. At movie theaters, third level price discrimination, which is based on age, favors teens and senior citizens, consequently discriminating against the customers who do not belong to these specific age groups.

The key to making price discrimination work (and doing so legally) is to use a more implicit form of discrimination. Frequently, businesses input a provision into the offer that makes it very unattractive to one segment but not to another segment. Various forms of third level price discrimination can border on or be illegal, but many forms are legal and acceptable, such as granting lower prices to senior citizens and disabled people.

Dynamic Pricing is a variation of the discrimination pricing tactic. In this variation, the business rapidly modifies and adjusts the prices for individual customers according to individual customers' characteristics. For example, in the early 2000s, the Wall Street Journal newspaper uncovered that Amazon, a United States-based online commerce company, had practiced first level pricing discrimination by applying dynamic pricing on the amazon.com website. Amazon presented different customers with different prices for the same item, and those uniquely individual prices were calculated according to the specific customer's past spending. This meant that Amazon presented higher prices to customers who spent more money on Amazon. Amazon quickly stopped practicing dynamic pricing once it became public knowledge.

Demand-based Pricing is another variation of the discrimination pricing tactic, applied by rapidly adjusting the prices for individual customers according to market characteristics. For example, in the late 1990s, Coca-Cola tested a vending machine that could automatically raise prices for its drinks in hot weather. Coca-Cola implemented a process, which constitutes demand-based pricing, through a temperature sensor and a computer chip. The company's chairman and chief executive officer, Douglas Ivester, heralded the revenue potential of using demand-based pricing. The New York Times quoted Ivester as saying that "The desire for a cold drink can increase during a sports championship final held in the summer heat. So, it is fair that is should be more expensive. The machine will simply make this process automatic." In the end, Coca-Cola did not pursue or implement demand-based pricing in its vending machines.

4.21 Maturity and Decline Life Cycle Stages

During the maturity and decline life cycle stage, you can apply two types of pricing tactics to the base price: initiatives and reactions.

The *Initiatives* pricing tactic is comprised of two methods: reductions and bundling. *Reductions* are universal, non-discriminatory, and non-conditional official list price decreases. The objective in using reductions is to increase demand and appeal to low-income segments. The disadvantage is a devaluation of the product, signaling that the product is in the decline stage.

Note that price reductions are permanent, but discounts are a temporary and conditional measure.

Bundling is creating a set of products that are coupled or packaged together to form a new unified offering, with the price of the combined set of products being lower than the total prices of the individual products. In more concise terms, bundling occurs when a business sells multiple products together, but the bundle is priced lower than the sum of the products' prices.

Bundling offers greater collective value, but the disadvantage is diffusion of any of the combined products' individual value and branding.

Direct Bundling is a type of bundling where the customer must buy the entire package. This is the most common type of bundling and is demonstrated by the combination meals (a.k.a. combo meals) at McDonalds, where the customer orders a meal, which usually consists of a main course, side order, and drink (e.g. hamburger, French fries, and soda).

Indirect Bundling is a type of virtual bundling where the seller does not physically package products together. Instead, the customer cannot buy product X without also buying product Y, in fixed proportions. The business can very quickly implement or remove this type of bundling. It is commonly used in retail stores such as supermarkets. For example, one package of cheese is conditionally available for purchase only if the customer buys one carton of milk—usually (but not necessarily) the bundled products come from the same manufacturer.

Certain conditions must be in place for successful bundling. These include the following:

- Customers must be able to buy bundle components individually.
- Customer groups have inversely related preferences.
- The bundle's components do not compete with each other.
- The vendor has knowledge of the customer valuation of the bundle components.

The *Reactions* pricing tactic can constitute literally any pricing method that attempts to extend the duration of the product's maturity life cycle stage and prevent or delay that product's decline life cycle stage.

4.22 Pricing Formula

The *Pricing Formula* stage in the MVP Model describes the calculatory structure that allows the application of pricing changes to specific markets or competitive regions.

The pricing formula contains three elements that allow price manipulations: variables, discounts, and licensing. (Fig. 4.10).

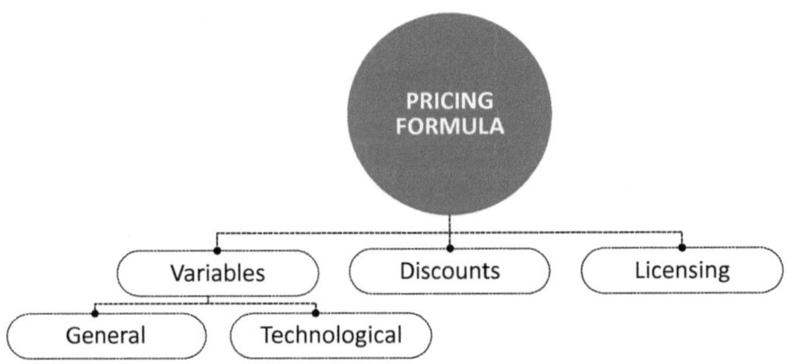

Fig. 4.10 Pricing formula stage in the MVP model

The *Variables* element is price changes that are based on product characteristics. With this element, you can use two types of pricing variables: general pricing variables and technological pricing variables.

The *General Pricing Variables* element commonly bases alterations to the price on non-technical parameters, such as scale (number of users of the product), schedule (pace of project completion), implementation challenges (any unique implementation issues), or transactions (number of transactions—usually found in e-commerce applications).

The *Technological Pricing Variables* element commonly bases alterations to the price on technical parameters, such as security issues (companies have different levels of security needs and different preferences when it comes to security), remote management (charges can be presented if a company demands additional or complex management layers), or reserved capacity (some clients need guaranteed service levels in terms of performance and response times).

The *Discounts* element uses conditional and temporary deductions from the official list price. There are three common types of discounts: modifiers, allowances, and global discounts.

Modifiers are conditional deductions from the list price. Common types of modifiers include cash, volume, and time frame deductions. *Cash* deductions hinge on an immediate payment via a bank note or check. *Volume* deductions depend on the customer making a large quantity purchase. *Time frame* deductions are granted when a purchase is made within a prescribed time or calendar period.

Allowances are also conditional refunds, but only in the form of deductions from the list price in exchange for customer action. The most common types of allowances are the trade-in and rebate. With the *Trade-in* option, the customer gives an item of property to the seller as part of the payment upon making a purchase. A *Rebate* constitutes reimbursement for a portion of the purchase price in exchange for customer information (e.g. completing a questionnaire).

Usually, the product's manufacturer is responsible for and grants the rebate. Rebates ensure a discount by giving money directly from the manufacturer to the customer, and they gather market intelligence.

The *Upgrade* option is a special form of trade-in. In an upgrade, the seller grants a reduced price of new product releases for current customers of older product versions in order to maintain customer loyalty. It is essentially the trade-in option, but the item of property is an older version of the product that is being purchased.

The *Competitive Upgrade* is yet another form of trade-in that grants a reduced price of a new product. In this type of upgrade, however, the buyer relinquishes the license or ownership to a competing product. The competitive upgrade option can be a very rewarding mechanism to the product's manufacturer, since it simultaneously generates revenue and increases market share while decreasing the competition's market share. Some vendors disallow competitive upgrade action to their own products through a legal clause in the *End User License Agreement* (EULA). This removes the possibility of having their products subjected to competitive upgrade action.

Global Discounts are temporary, universal, non-discriminatory, non-conditional deductions from the list price for enticement purposes.

The main advantage of discounting is that it quickly increases market share. However, discounting can have negative implications as it can devalue the product, may cause price wars, can inherently have a short-term effect, and can create discount-prone customers. As such, it is generally recommended that you do not devalue your products by lowering prices to entice sales. Alternately, it is recommended you promote your higher value products with higher profit margins through marketing.

Licensing is a vendor's option that allows variations in rights to usage and ownership and a means of granting usage and ownership rights. Businesses always request more money when giving more usage and ownership rights.

Licensing impacts the way in which Total Cost of Ownership (TCO) is presented to the buyer, but it is only cosmetic, as the seller ultimately formulates the licensing parameters to achieve a certain margin or profit.

The following are different types of licensing fees:

- *One-Time Fee*—one-time fixed charge that enables constant use of the product
- *Subscription Fee*—one-time fixed charge that enables limited time use of the product (a.k.a. registration fee, activation fee, or setup fee)
- *Recurring Fee*—fixed charge that enables limited time use of the product, but is renewed periodically at regular intervals
- *Usage Fee*—charge per unit of measure that is tallied at regular intervals

The licensing alternatives include a perpetual or conditional license. A *Perpetual License* grants non-expiring ownership and usage rights to a product. With a *Conditional License*, ownership and usage rights to a product expire (a.k.a. term license) and can be either renewable or non-renewable.

The *Licensing Mix* is a term applied to a combination of perpetual and term licenses relative to a particular product.

A perpetual license is often based on a one-time fee and is often applied to a tangible product (goods). The term license is often based on recurring fees and applied to an intangible product (services).

A business can apply licensing fees individually or in combination and can complement or substitute a base price.

For example, consumer electronics are overwhelmingly sold with a perpetual license and a one-time fee. Services such as club memberships and cable televisions are sold with a licensing mix comprised of a subscription fee and a recurring fee. Utility companies sell residential electrical power and water with a licensing mix that includes a subscription fee and a usage fee.

Many cellular/mobile communication operators employ a licensing mix that includes a combination of licensing fees. For example, the operators charge a one-time fee for purchasing the mobile phone, a subscription fee in the form of a service activation fee, a recurring fee as a monthly maintenance charge, and a usage fee for the air time minutes.

4.23 Pricing Formula Retention Drill

1. Which are the three major components of the Pricing Formula?
   (a) Modifiers, Discounts, Licensing
   (b) Discounts, Modifiers, Allowances
   (c) Costs, Inclusions, Reductions
   (d) Variables, Discounts, Licensing
2. What is the objective and description of the Variables component of the Pricing Formula?
   (a) Deductions from the list price
   (b) Variations in rights to usage and ownership
   (c) Calculatory structure for pricing adjustments
   (d) Price changes based on product attributes
3. What is the objective and description of the Discounts component of the Pricing Formula?
   (a) Price changes based on product attributes
   (b) Deductions from the list price
   (c) Variations in rights to usage and ownership
   (d) Calculatory structure for pricing adjustments
4. What is the objective and description of the Licensing component of the Pricing Formula?
   (a) Price changes based on product attributes
   (b) Variations in rights to usage and ownership
   (c) Deductions from the list price
   (d) Calculatory structure for pricing adjustments

Answers: 1-(d), 2-(d), 3-(b), 4-(b)

4.24 Price Mix

The *Price Mix* stage in the MVP Model describes the price-related combination of information and conditions that the company presents to the customer.

The price mix contains four elements: MSRP, adjustments, monetary, and contract (Fig. 4.11).

The *Manufacturer's Suggested Retail Price* (MSRP) element is the official published price the manufacturer recommends that the seller offers the product for. The MSRP helps to standardize prices among locations. While some sellers always sell at below the suggested retail price, others do so only when they place items on sale or clearance.

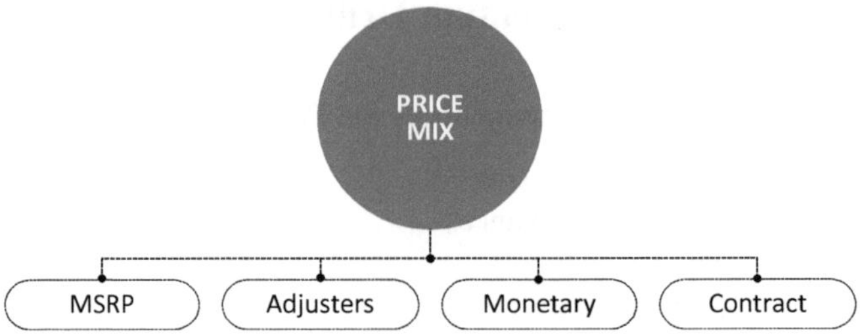

Fig. 4.11 Price mix stage in the MVP model

The *Adjusters* element is a group of partial influencers which alter the MSRP according to a given situation or condition. The partial influencers include variables, discounts, tax, and shipping.

The *Variables* are price changes based on product characteristics (e.g. the number of users permitted to access a software application).

Discounts are temporary conditional deductions from the list price (e.g. an early-bird discount—a reduced price if the customer makes payment before a specific date).

Monetary is a subgroup of partial influencers that include *Payment Forms*, which are a means of payment such as cash, credit card, check, or wire transfer. *Payment Terms* are the payment conditions, such as currency type, letter of credit (promissory note in which a bank pledges to provide a financial loan), and purchase prerequisites. *Credit Terms* are a schedule for delayed payment/s. For example, the monetary section of the price mix can reflect payment when a product is accepted via credit card only, in United States dollars, and with the option of paying in three equal installments over a three-month period.

Contract is a subgroup of partial influencers that includes the *End User License Agreement* (EULA), which is a legal and binding contract that sets the parameters of usage and ownership rights granted to the customer. *Terms and Conditions* set the requirements and obligations of the parties. A vendor issues a *Disclaimer* as a legal denial of responsibility to any events in order to discourage legal action by the customer.

In lay terms, the EULA describes what the customer is allowed and not allowed to do with the product. The terms and conditions describe the seller's obligations to the customer and vice versa. The disclaimer legally states that the vendor has no responsibility to any negative events that may arise from using the product.

4.25 Price Mix Retention Drill

1. Which are the four major components of the Price Mix?

   (a) Variables, Adjusters, Monetary, MSRP

(b) Monetary, Licensing, Modifiers, Contract
(c) MSRP, Adjusters, Monetary, Contract
(d) Monetary, MSRP, Allowances, Legal

2. What is the objective and description of the MSRP component of the Price Mix?

(a) Variations to the MSRP
(b) Payment terms and conditions
(c) Manufacturer's suggested retail price
(d) Granted rights to usage and ownership

3. What is the objective and description of the Adjusters component of the Price Mix?

(a) Variations to the MSRP
(b) Manufacturer's suggested retail price
(c) Payment terms and conditions
(d) Granted rights to usage and ownership

4. What is the objective and description of the Monetary component of the Price Mix?

(a) Manufacturer's suggested retail price
(b) Payment terms and conditions
(c) Variations to the MSRP
(d) Granted rights to usage and ownership

5. What is the objective and description of the Contract component of the Price Mix?

(a) Manufacturer's suggested retail price
(b) Variations to the MSRP
(c) Granted rights to usage and ownership
(d) Payment terms and conditions

Answers: 1-(c), 2-(c), 3-(a), 4-(b), 5-(c)

Chapter 5
Blackblot Market-Value Pricing™ Model Glossary

Clear definitions that establish a common understanding, better internal cooperation, and standard corporate processes.

5.1 MVP Model Glossary Description

Perspectives abound as to how to define the terms associated with pricing. These interpretations vary significantly to a point where pricing fundamentals are interpreted very differently by different companies. This diversity also influences the professional terminology that shapes corporate pricing processes.

Therefore, clear definitions are useful to help establish a common understanding. The following are term definitions as they are used throughout the *Blackblot Market-Value Pricing™ Model* (MVP Model).

5.2 MVP Model Glossary

Blackblot term	Blackblot Market-Value Pricing™ model definition
Actual relative value	The ratio of benefits and costs[customer] the product factually delivers to customers
Actual resultant value	A fixed combination of gains in time, cost, and status the product factually delivers to customers
Actual value	The measured and validated worth that the customer or similar customers factually obtain from owning and using the product
Actual value formula	*Actual value = actual resultant value + actual relative value*

(continued)

G. Steinhardt, *Market-Value Pricing*, SpringerBriefs in Business,
https://doi.org/10.1007/978-3-030-10734-5_5

Blackblot term	Blackblot Market-Value Pricing™ model definition
Allowances (Pricing)	A conditional refund in the form of a deduction from the list price in exchange for customer action; Allowances are often accomplished in two forms: Trade-in (pricing)—an item of property given in part payment upon purchase; Rebate (pricing)—customer receives reimbursement for a portion of the purchase price, in exchange for customer information
Bait pricing	Pricing that aims to attract customers with low prices with intent to sell higher-priced items
Base price	The initial price of a product before any alteration
Benefits	Product features that are desirable to the customer
Business strategy	Decisions that support being a leader, follower, or innovator in a specific line of business
Business-to-Business (B2B)	The transaction of goods or services between businesses
Business-to-Consumer (B2C)	The transaction of goods or services between businesses and private individuals
Buyer	The entity that decides to obtain the product
Captive product (Pricing tactic)	An imbalanced price ratio between a product's components which are sold separately; The main system component is underpriced, and the consumables or support services are overpriced; The captive product pricing tactic can be quickly and easily accomplished via product system decoupling
Client	The entity that is the receiver of goods or services
Conditional license	Expiring ownership and usage rights to a product; can be renewable and non-renewable
Consumer	An individual or household that buys and uses goods and services created by industries
Consumer products	Products intended for use by household consumers for non-business purposes Consumer Products are used for personal gain
Costs[Customer]	The aggregate expenses incurred by the customer from buying and using the product (essentially Total Cost of Ownership or TCO)
Credit terms	Schedule for delayed payment/s
Demand (Economics)	Quantity of a product that will be bought in the market at various prices for a specified period
Demand-based pricing (Pricing tactic)	Rapidly adjusting prices per customer according to market characteristics
Derived price	Price that is determined based on attributed benefit
Disclaimer	Denial of responsibility for events occurring during product ownership to discourage current or future legal action
Discrimination (Pricing tactic)	Charging different market segments different prices for the same product There are several levels of discrimination: • First level—price discrimination that is based on the ability to pay (charge-per-income) • Second level—price discrimination that is based on artificial obstacles (same price yet coupons, advance purchase, restricted use) • Third level—price discrimination that is based on external factors (gender, age, geography, or profession)

(continued)

Blackblot term	Blackblot Market-Value Pricing™ model definition
Diversification (Pricing tactic)	Creating product variants with distributed price points
Dynamic pricing (Pricing tactic)	Rapidly adjusting prices per customer according to customer characteristics
End User License Agreement (EULA)	Perimeters of usage and ownership rights granted to the customer
Global discount	Universal, non-discriminatory, non-conditional deduction from the list price, for enticement purposes
Innovation formula	*Innovation = invention + utilization*
Licensing	A method of providing rights to usage and ownership to a product, for a specified price and/or term
Licensing mix	A combination of perpetual and term licenses relative to a particular product
Loss leader	A product that is priced below cost to attract consumers to buy other items
Margins	Direct financial gains by selling
MSRP	Manufacturer's suggested retail price; the price the manufacturer recommends that the seller offers the product for
MVP model	A market-value centric pricing process which guides sets of managerial decisions that help determine a product's price The *Blackblot Market-Value Pricing™ Model* is comprised of three distinct components that effectively act as sequential stages in the pricing process: pricing scheme, pricing formula, and price mix
Odd/Even pricing	Ending the price with certain numbers to influence buyers' perceptions of the price or product
One-time fee (Licensing)	A one-time fixed charge that enables constant use of the product
Payment	The actual economic sacrifice a customer makes to acquire certain rights to a product
Payment forms	Means of payment such as cash, credit card, check, or wire transfer
Payment terms	Payment conditions such as currency type, letter of credit and purchase prerequisites
Penetration (Pricing tactic)	Briefly charging a relatively low price upon product launch
Perceived value	An unsubstantiated estimation of worth that the customer obtains or could potentially obtain from owning and using the product
Perceived value formula	*Perceived value = resultant value proposition + relative value proposition*
Perpetual license	Non-expiring ownership and usage rights to a product
Price	A specification of what a seller wants in exchange for granting right of ownership or use to a product. The price formula is *Price = costs + margins*
Price discounts	Deductions from the list price
Price elasticity of demand	Percentage change in quantity demanded that occurs in response to a percentage change in price
Price lining	Pricing of products in a product family with corresponding price points
Price mix	A price-related aggregate of information and conditions that the customer is presented with

(continued)

Blackblot term	Blackblot Market-Value Pricing™ model definition
Price modifiers	Conditional deduction from the list price
Price psychology	Dynamic human reasoning process which infers from a product's price, price comparisons, and price changes, diverse messages about the product and company, and accordingly influences buying decisions
Price reductions	Universal, non-discriminatory, and non-conditional official list price decreases
Price variables	Price changes based on product characteristics
Pricing	The act of setting a price
Pricing formula	A calculative structure that allows the application of pricing changes to specific markets or competitive regions
Pricing objectives	A description of what a company wants to achieve through pricing its products
Pricing scheme	An outline of the overall pricing approach which encompasses the principles for pricing the specific product
Pricing strategy	The primary method to pricing that relies on a particular pricing decision factor
Pricing tactics	Pricing actions which are dependent on the particular life cycle stage of the product that is being priced
Product bundling	An aggregate of products sold collectively at a price that is lower than the sum of their prices; The price of the set of products is lower than the total of individual products; Bundling is often accomplished in two forms: • Direct bundling—customer must buy the entire package • Indirect bundling—customer cannot buy product X without also buying Y, in fixed proportions
Product portfolio	A product line in which the products are properly diversified and balanced along the timeline and stages of the product life cycle model
Recurring fee (Licensing)	A fixed charge that enables limited time use of the product, but is renewed periodically at regular intervals
Relative value proposition	An implicit promise a product holds for customers to deliver a desired ratio of benefits and costs[customer]
Resultant value proposition	An implicit promise a product holds for customers to deliver a fixed combination of gains in time, cost, and status
Seller	The entity that sells the product or service
Site license discount	Discount provided to a large quantity purchase; The number of product licenses acquired is estimated
Skimming (Pricing tactic)	Briefly charging a relatively high price upon product launch
Subscription fee (Licensing)	A one-time fixed charge that enables limited time use of the product
Superior perceived value	A state where customers perceive the product gives a net value more positive than its alternatives
Superior perceived value formula	*Superior perceived value = competitive advantage + value*
Supply	Quantity of a product that will be offered to the market by suppliers at various prices for a specific period

(continued)

Blackblot term	Blackblot Market-Value Pricing™ model definition
Target market/s	The group or groups of customers selected by a firm to sell to
Unique Selling Proposition (USP)	A key statement that describes the distinct and compelling value of the product, which sets the product apart from other competing products
Usage fee (Licensing)	A charge per unit of measure that is tallied at regular intervals
User	The entity that interacts with the product
Value	The worth derived by the customer from owning and using the product
Value formula	$Value = benefits - costs[customer]$
Volume price (Discount)	Discount provided to a large quantity purchase; The exact number of product licenses acquired is stated

Chapter 6
Blackblot Market-Value Pricing™ (MVP) Model

6.1 Blackblot Market-Value Pricing™ Model Description

Developed by Blackblot, the *Blackblot Market-Value Pricing™ Model* (MVP Model) is a market-value centric pricing process which guides sets of managerial decisions that help determine a product's price. *Price* is the specification of what a seller wants in exchange for granting right of ownership or use to a product. *Pricing* is the act of setting a price.

The *MVP Model* is comprised of three distinct parts that effectively act as sequential stages in the pricing process:

1. *Pricing Scheme*—outline of the overall pricing approach which encompasses the principles for pricing the specific product (how to achieve)
2. *Pricing Formula*—calculative structure that allows the application of pricing changes to specific markets or competitive regions (how to calculate)
3. *Price Mix*—price-related aggregate of information and conditions that the customer is presented with (how to present)

The *MVP Model* is designed to be used in conjunction with the *MVP Pricing Model* spreadsheet and the *MVP Pricing Model* template.

G. Steinhardt, *Market-Value Pricing*, SpringerBriefs in Business,
https://doi.org/10.1007/978-3-030-10734-5_6

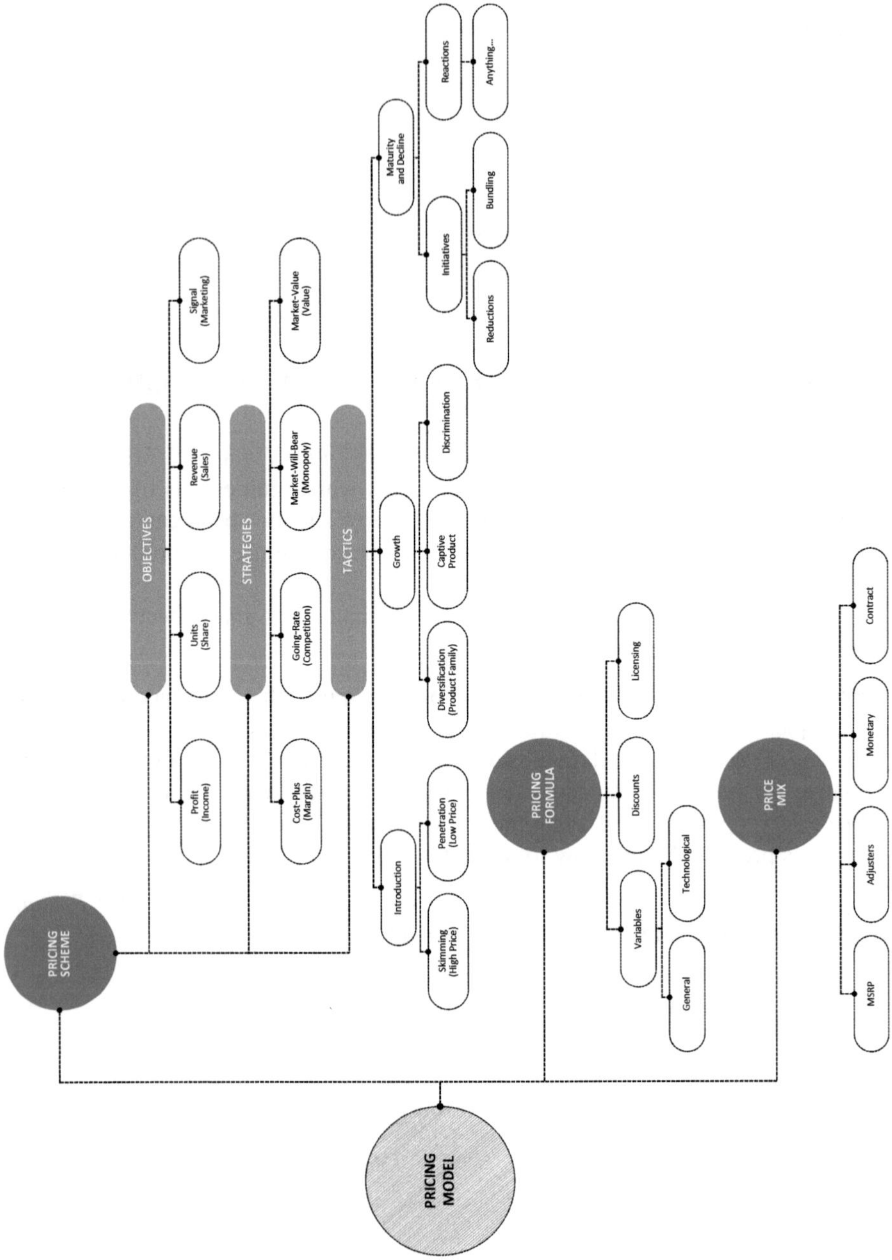
PRICING MODEL
PRICING SCHEME
OBJECTIVES
Profit (Income)
Units (Share)
Revenue (Sales)
Signal (Marketing)
STRATEGIES
Cost-Plus (Margin)
Going-Rate (Competition)
Market-Will-Bear (Monopoly)
Market-Value (Value)
TACTICS
Introduction
Skimming (High Price)
Penetration (Low Price)
Growth
Diversification (Product Family)
Captive Product
Discrimination
Maturity and Decline
Initiatives
Reductions
Bundling
Reactions
Anything...
PRICING FORMULA
Variables
General
Technological
Discounts
Licensing
PRICE MIX
MSRP
Adjusters
Monetary
Contract

MIX
Papier aus verantwortungsvollen Quellen
Paper from responsible sources
FSC® C105338

If you have any concerns about our products,
you can contact us on
ProductSafety@springernature.com

In case Publisher is established outside the EU,
the EU authorized representative is:
Springer Nature Customer Service Center GmbH
Europaplatz 3, 69115 Heidelberg, Germany

Printed by Libri Plureos GmbH
in Hamburg, Germany